DEDICATION

My faith to the Man upstairs for providing strength and guidance. My appreciation and love to my family for putting up with the risks, time and commitment that was required to get the company to this point. My thanks to my business partners for believing that we could make a positive difference in what appears to be a world of increased cultural, ethnic and social divisiveness.

M2R
Metrics2Results

https://facebook.com//Metrics2Results/

https://twitter.com/Metrics2Results

https://linkedin.com/company/10690106

Metrics2Results.blogspot.com

Metrics2Results.com

1

"We naturally assign people into various social categories divided by salient and chronically accessible traits, such as age, gender, race, and role. And just as we might have implicit cognitions that help us walk and drive, we have social cognitions that guide our thinking about social categories. Where do these schemas come from? They come from our experiences with other people, some of them direct (i.e., real-world encounters) but most of them vicarious (i.e., relayed to us through stories, books, movies, media, and culture)" …….

Jerry Kang, Vice Chancellor for Equity, Diversity and Inclusion – UCLA

"Rather than judging, condemning and excluding the person who has said something inappropriate, I suggest examining these incidents through the lens of unconscious bias. Because prejudice (a pre-judgement of somebody or something) often originates from the sub-conscious, the person is probably unaware of having the judgement in the first place, unless we encourage them to explore the incident further."

Sarah Cornally, Founding Partner - Academy of System Dynamics

"A Few Key Characteristics of Implicit Biases
- *Implicit Biases are **pervasive...***
- *Implicit and explicit biases are **related but distinct mental constructs...***
- *The implicit associations we hold **do not necessarily align with our declared beliefs...***
- *We generally tend to hold implicit biases that **favor our own ingroup...***
- *Implicit biases are **malleable.** Our brains are incredibly complex, and the implicit associations that we have formed can be gradually unlearned through a variety of techniques"*

Kirwan Institute – Ohio State University

TABLE OF CONTENTS

To the reader:
This book is written in a manner for you to read the chapters in any order you wish.

Chapter 1: Introduction

As a society, we have grown accustomed to the concept of "sizing up" someone as quickly as possible. Unfortunately, many times, this sizing up process is based on first impressions and outer-appearance. Both are guided significantly by our unconscious (implicit) bias. These biases, many times, are based on inaccurate or false information or input. That false or inaccurate information can create several behaviors such as stereotyping, hatred, prejudice, and other unfavorable behaviors. It can also create unfavorable behavioral responses to events and situations that occur such as rioting, terrorism, and other unfavorable behaviors.

As discussed throughout the chapters of the book, our early environments and our individual experiences with others, situations and events have placed certain implicit biases in all of us. These unconscious biases create beliefs for us, and those beliefs color our views of the world around us. We call those views "filters." These filters control our behaviors when interacting with others and our initial reaction to situations and events.

Our hope, and goal, is to help:

- develop a better understanding of these implicit biases, and
- determine whether they create favorable or unfavorable behaviors for us.

Once that is determined it is up to each of us, individually, to decide our future behaviors. This process is "Turning Unconscious Bias into Conscious Thought."

$$E + E = BBF$$

BEHAVIOR

(Our interaction with others; Our reactions to situations and events)

Chapter 2: You & I

I have mentally wrestled with the whole concept of unconscious bias, or also known as implicit bias, being fact or fiction. It was initially difficult for me to grasp how something that occurs in my sub-conscious could have such an impact on my interaction with others; and my reactions to situations and events. I, and perhaps you, have always considered myself a rational thinker and rational decision-maker. However, the more we studied implicit bias; the more I began to realize the large role these unconscious biases play in our thought processes.

One of the key breakthroughs for me was the research we did regarding the speed of unconscious thought versus conscious thinking. Scientists and psychologists have varying theories on the actual difference in speed between conscious and subconscious thought. However, there is a consensus that the unconscious is extremely faster than our conscious thought. There are hundreds of articles available regarding the unbelievable speed of unconscious thought.

When our brain is building the mental databases for unconscious thinking and our unconscious decision-making process, it is primarily drawing from the influences and inputs from our early environments and our individual experiences.

As an example, have you ever driven somewhere and only remember parts of the trip? This is a common experience. The parts of the trip we don't remember can be attributed to our unconscious mind taking control: recognizing traffic signals; stop signs; a familiar route; traffic around us, etc. This same experience of our unconscious mind taking control can occur when we are interacting with others, or reacting to situations or events.

Our unconscious mind will think and react much faster, and pull information from our past environment and/or experiences and prompt us to take a course of immediate response or action. This is useful when you are driving a vehicle, but may not be as beneficial in interactions with people or responses to situations and events. This might be an issue if the input that is guiding our unconscious response or reaction is false or inaccurate.

Think about the times you have responded to someone, or a situation, that you wish you could rewind and do differently? In many cases, our initial response is driven by our unconscious thinking, and we may respond too quickly. So, what occurs if the unconscious mind has false or inaccurate data from our early environments or our experiences?

Chapter 3: Home

I was raised in a small community in Southwestern Michigan. I grew up in a home where my father was the bread-winner, and my mother did not work outside the home. The area was known for its many lakes. How does all of this relate to implicit bias? What does it have to do with the development of beliefs that influenced my view of people, events, and situations?

Let's start with the fact that my father worked outside the home, and my mother did not. Unconsciously, the home environment I grew up in defined my belief in male/female relationships and the role for each. Additionally, it shaped my view that the female did not work outside the home and the male was the bread-winner. What would happen if I didn't recognize the implicit bias created by my home environment regarding male/female roles?

How might that affect me today as a subordinate, co-worker or manager of females? What about my possible thoughts and behavior towards them in the workforce? If I made decisions based on my implicit bias, my work behavior towards women could be significantly affected.

As a subordinate, I might not respect or appreciate receiving work direction from a female manager. As a co-worker, I might treat them differently from my male counterparts. As their manager, I might treat their wages; performances reviews; and promotions differently than males. You can probably see through these examples why it is so critically important to recognize our implicit biases, and convert them to conscious thoughts that better guide our decision-making processes.

What if my home environment created an implicit (unconscious) bias for me that women, especially with children, should not work outside the home? It might also infer that if they do work outside the home, I may believe their value, in the workforce, is less than males. This could result in several possible undesired behaviors: paying female associates less than their male counterparts; a preference of promoting males versus females; providing higher performance review ratings for men; having more social engagement and extra-curricular activities with the men in my organization; Etc.

What if your organization, or even your industry or market, was perceived to provide preferential treatment to males? How many high-talent females do you think your organization would attract or be able to recruit? What if women in your organization thought that promotions were a privilege reserved for males? How long do you think the high-talent females would stay in the organization?

NOTE: *Here are some interesting points*

- *The U.S. Bureau of Labor Statistics estimates that females make up 47% of today's workforce.*
- *Additionally, the National Center for Education Statistics estimated that females were 57% of the 2016 U.S. college and university enrollment population.*
- *Based on U.S. Census Bureau data, females make up approximately 51% of the U.S. population.*

The combination of this data would suggest a continued increasing rate in the number of females entering the workforce over the next several years.

In another story about the home environment, we had a young female participant in one our workshops. She described a home environment where she was mistreated and then abandoned by her father. Because of this, she had developed a major distrust for him. Unfortunately, as she began to process through her beliefs (turning unconscious bias into conscious thought) she realized that her distrust not only applied to her father; it had become a distrust towards all males.

So, as it relates to males, how could this implicit bias affect her behavior professionally and personally? How do you think her distrust towards men affected behavior in her relationships with male associates, male managers, and even male clients? It was extremely humbling to watch this young lady turn unconscious bias into conscious thought, and begin to identify some of the beliefs and behaviors she had developed from those biases.

Mistrust of males may not be your implicit bias. However, the point of the example is to ask you think through your own early environments. We want you to explore and understand what root causes may have led you to develop your unconscious biases; and more importantly what impact those biases have on your current behaviors, interactions with others, and your reaction to situations and events.

NOTE: *Here are some interesting points*

- *Nearly 700,000 children are abused in the U.S annually. An estimated 683,000 children (unique incidents) were victims of abuse and neglect in 2015, the most recent year for which there is national data.*
  Source:
  http://www.nationalchildrensalliance.org/media-room/media-kit/national-statistics-child-abuse
- *1 in 5 women and 1 in 71 men in the United States has been raped in their lifetime. Source:* http://ncadv.org/learn-more/statistics
- *72% of all murder-suicides involve an intimate partner; 94% of the victims of these murder-suicides are female. Source:* http://ncadv.org/learn-more/statistics

Your home environment may have many other things that affected your implicit biases and beliefs. However, it is strongly believed in psychology circles that the following have a significant impact on the development of our beliefs and implicit biases:

✓ What we are taught
✓ What we observe
✓ What we participate in
✓ What form of punishment and the reasons for punishment

✓ What types of rewards and the reasons for reward.

These might be some of the questions that we ask ourselves about the learned beliefs and behaviors from our early environments:

Are my biases based on fact or fiction?

Are they based on stereotypes, misleading information, or opinions?

Are they based on someone else's beliefs that have been passed down to me?

Chapter 4: Neighborhood

As I wrote in Chapter 3, I grew up in a rural environment in Michigan; directly across the state border with Indiana. The population in this region of the United States is primarily a mixture of Caucasian, Black, and Latino (primarily Mexican).

In addition to Protestant and Catholic religious denominations, the area also included Amish, Mennonite and Muslim groups. During the Viet Nam war era, several Vietnamese refugees relocated to this area. Also, people from the surrounding larger cities, primarily Detroit and Chicago, either relocated here or spent their summers. My point to all of this is that I grew up in an area that provided a rich environment for observing others; and interacting with many different types of people. This neighborhood of diverse people and various beliefs was the beginning of my observations as it relates to unconscious, or implicit, bias.

I can so vividly remember the many fruit and vegetable farms that had migrant workers harvesting their crops. I can still see the Amish wagons being pulled by horses on paved highways. I can hear the very broken English spoken by many of the Mexican migrant workers and the war-era refugees. I can remember the members of the Black Muslim faith and the women wearing their hair covered; and the men in their small hats. So, what has all this to do with implicit bias?

I will discuss many of these groups in other chapters in the book. However, for this chapter let's discuss the migrant workers. The majority were from Mexico. As I think through my early exposure to them, I realize that I established many unconscious biases that created early beliefs for me regarding Mexicans:

- They were nomadic people; unable to remain in a single location for long-term periods
- They were great workers, but were rarely put in leadership positions
- They didn't care much about material things; they preferred a more meager lifestyle

Think about these biases and beliefs that I developed early about the Mexican population. If I did not convert these to conscious thought, how could they have affected my current behavior? What if I happened to be the supervisor, or manager, of Mexican associates.

What if I still believed that they could not stay in one location for a long period of time? Do you think I would consider placing them in a job or position that required a long-term commitment?

What if I believed they were great workers, but probably would not make good leaders? Do you think that I would be eager to promote them?

What if I thought they were more content with a meager life.? Is it possible that I would pay them less than others because they don't expect the same pay and would readily accept less than others?

If we don't convert our unconscious biases into conscious thought, they will shape our beliefs of others and our initial reactions to situations and events. Whatever those beliefs may be, they will shape how we view the world and create behaviors and responses based on those beliefs: Whether those behaviors are favorable or unfavorable.

Just like my neighborhood experience with the Mexican people. Had I not taken the time to review my early experiences with them, I might not have recognized my unfavorable biases, beliefs and possible behaviors towards them.

In a recent workshop, we had a young White/Caucasian male that grew up in an urban environment. In his neighborhood, most of the population were people of color; primarily Black/African-Americans. One of his beliefs that he expressed in the workshop was Black/African-American males do not hold the value of family in high regard. Based on his neighborhood environment, he observed that Black/African American males would have children and many times abandon their spouse and their children.

During the discussion regarding his neighborhood experience, he realized that he held a belief and unconscious bias that extended beyond his neighborhood. He now, unconsciously, related this neighborhood experience to his belief about the entire Black/African-American male population. As he began to process this bias consciously, he began to understand its impact on his current day behaviors.

The biggest "aha" moment for him was his behavior of stereotyping and prejudging an entire group of people based on a small sub-section of that group. He realized that his current interaction, with Black/African-American males, was extremely different than his interactions with others.

Think about the impact of these types of beliefs and biases that we apply to an entire group of people, based on our exposure to a small subset of our neighborhood environment. How could it affect our social interaction with them? How could it affect our behavior if a member of this group decided to move into our neighborhood today? How could it affect our behavior, and response, as parents if one of our children brought a visitor to our home that belonged to a group that we hold these beliefs and biases towards?

Chapter 5: Culture

"Culture is the characteristics and knowledge of a particular group of people, defined by everything from language, religion, cuisine, social habits, music, and arts…"
Kim Ann Zimmermann, Live Science Contributor

The home I grew up in was situated on an acre of land adjacent to a lake. This setting made our house the gathering place during the summer for parties, picnics and just good old-fashioned get-togethers. It was not unusual for large groups of people to attend these events. However, I did notice a considerable difference when the group consisted of people that looked like me versus other times when the groups were racially and ethnically diverse.

When events were attended primarily by people who looked like me, the conversations and tone were considerably more open and relaxed. Conversations and relationships between the attendees seem to be much more jovial and close. This observation occurred for me very early in life. What I didn't understand was that this was part of my family's culture.

A culture built around a deep trust and fellowship with those that looked like us; and a culture of creating a "safe distance" relationship with those that did not. This created an implicit bias in my adult years that took me considerable time to recognize its effect on my beliefs and behaviors.

One noticeable effect on my behavior was the fact that I would always greet people that looked like me, no matter where I was. I could be in stores, airports, meetings, or even just walking down the street. It was my way of always acknowledging the closeness and trust I thought we had: even if I knew nothing about the other person. As I begin to recognize this behavior, and its root cause, I began to question the validity of feeling relational closeness and trust with total strangers.

This is an example of how implicit biases can lead to behaviors that have no grounding in fact or reality. I am sure those strangers I always greeted who looked like me, were no different than those strangers who didn't look like me. They were all people that I didn't know, or have any real relationship connection.

However, my early cultural environment taught me to place more trust in those that looked like me versus those who didn't. It taught me culturally that I had more in common with those whose outer appearance was like mine versus those who looked different.

As I began to understand this unconscious bias, and its associated beliefs and behaviors, I realized that it was based on a "learned behavior." A behavior developed from observing my family's interaction with others in my earlier years. Behavior that had no basis in fact! A stranger that looks like me, or a stranger that doesn't look like me, are still just that... strangers!

Based on understanding the unconscious bias and beliefs that caused the original undesired behavior, I consciously made a behavioral change. Today, I am a total embarrassment to my children. I greet every person that I meet anywhere and anytime. This new behavior has led to many new acquaintances and a few new friends; personal and professional!

Today, we live in a Texas Metroplex recognized as one of the fastest growing areas in the United States. This period of growth and prosperity has attracted many different ethnic groups to a region whose history did not include large influxes of multi-cultural residents. The past few years have been interesting to observe the mixed reaction, especially the reactions of the longer-term residents.

Some of the longer-term residents have embraced the many changes that are occurring. Some are attempting to slow the migration of these cultures into their communities. Others have taken a more hostile approach with derogatory public and private comments and actions. Each of these groups of longer-term residents holds biases and filters (*their view of others, situations, and events*) based on their beliefs of what affect a multitude of cultural differences will have on them. Unfortunately, many of those unfavorable biases and behaviors are the result of inaccurate or false information.

I was talking with an East-Indian acquaintance that moved his family into the community about 14 years ago. Until now, he and his wife had never discussed moving back to India. However, because of recent unfavorable events, he is afraid for his family's safety and welfare. These recent events included written messages placed in his mailbox and verbal abuse from some in his neighborhood and community. Regardless of our beliefs, biases, and filters, prosperity and the ease of mobility will bring many more cultural differences to our communities.

These cultural shifts are visible in the types of restaurants, grocery stores, increased variety of sports, demographic changes in our school system populations and many other differences that generally occur in communities experiencing increased cultural diversity.

The questions are:

- What unconscious biases and behaviors have your beliefs caused, or could create, as it relates to multi-cultural environments?
- What unconscious biases and behaviors have your beliefs caused, or could create, as it relates to specific

cultures within a multi-cultural environment?

- What favorable or unfavorable behaviors do you exhibit when interacting with others, or responding to events or situations, related to cultures outside of your own?

Chapter 6: History

History has such a tremendous effect on each of our biases and beliefs. We believe there are some substantial reasons for this.

Depending on your ethnicity, your ancestor's experiences in early America will vary greatly. A country initially built on the pursuit of religious freedom and flight from unfair taxation, also is a country with a significant history of unrest:

A country where:

- o In a civil war early in its history, citizens were required to take the lives of other citizens.
- o For a short time, flew two separate flags.
- o Slavery, and a desire to keep free labor caused division even among the majority group.

- o Until relatively recent in USA history, women or people of color were not allowed to vote.
- o Some people supported a war and others were marching in the streets to stop it. Violent protests and even deaths on university campuses occurred.
- o Domestic and foreign terrorism shocked the Nation. Creating more divisiveness between those who favor isolationism versus those that want to maintain a world-view.

In the United States, there is a saying, "we all arrived here on different ships, but we're all in the same boat now!" The only problem is many of our historical milestones, like those listed above, have left to many implicit biases in their path; for too many people.

Some, in the Majority population, feel that it has been their knowledge and experience that has built this country. Some in the

Minority populations think they paid a horrible price, and sacrifice, to build this country. Some immigrants entering the country are wondering if they should fear, or be hopeful for, their future.

The common denominator in all of these scenarios is individual belief systems and the behaviors being driven by them. Our country's history has a considerable influence on each of our beliefs and the unconscious biases that lead to our favorable and unfavorable behaviors. History has also been a useful tool in changing unconscious bias into conscious thought. Let's use World War II as an example of history's impact.

Before World War II, there was a strong male bias that females were not suited to do specific jobs. Many women did not work outside the home, and when they did it was in specific functions such as nursing, teaching, secretaries, etc. These jobs at the time were considered situations that women could handle. Tasks such as executive positions, manufacturing jobs, heavy equipment operation, and maintenance, etc. were considered a job for men.

World War II created a high demand for workers. However, many of the men were called up to battle. This left a significant labor shortage for the "manly" jobs. Even though the biases still existed regarding women filling these positions; they not only filled the void for labor in those positions; they succeeded very well in them. Many of the unconscious biases regarding women in the workforce were changed for some; but not others. Many women remained in the workforce and began to advance into jobs previously considered, "for men only."

The unconscious bias towards females performing specific job functions has been rooted in the history of humankind for ages. The inclination of 'dominance" by the male population created this view of females being unable to fill specific roles in business. In fact, this implicit bias still exists in many industries, markets, and businesses today.

As we mentioned in Chapters 3 and 7, the ratio of women is increasing in the U.S population and the proportion of students attending universities. It is very feasible that females will continue to fill and succeed at more and more positions previously considered for the "Men's Club Only." They have proven that many of the beliefs that created the unconscious bias and behaviors towards them were based on fiction, not fact.

Another historical event that began to change unconscious biases were the civil rights movement activities in the 1960's and early 1970's. As it relates to the Black/African-American and the White/Caucasian population many beliefs, implicit biases, and filters existed on both sides.

Blacks and Whites have a longer history together in the U.S. than many of the other groups; except Indians/Native-Americans.

The relationship between Blacks and Whites has transitioned through many different levels:

- Master/Slave
- Boss/Indentured Servant
- Land Owner/Sharecropper
- Equal Citizens
- Co-Workers
- Neighbors
- Relatives

For both parties, many of the unconscious biases still exist based on recent, and not so recent, historical experiences. These experiences have created beliefs in both groups that have formed strong and unfavorable beliefs for many individuals in each of the groups. These deep beliefs and associated biases, particularly between whites and Blacks, have been a significant driver in the development of our interactive workshops.

As much as some of us like to believe we are color-blind, the fact is that color-blindness only exists if you are indeed a blind person without eyesight. Our workshops were developed to acknowledge race, ethnicity, mental disabilities, physical disabilities, and other outer-appearances can affect our views (filters) regarding others. This outer-appearance is what many of our competitors build their diversity "Multi-Cultural" training around. This type of training is an effort to increase tolerance; move towards embracing diversity, and understanding others.

As a company, we agree race and multi-cultural diversity brings strength to an organization through the differing ideas, opinions, backgrounds and other varying characteristics. However, some people feel like "diversity training" is being forced on them.

We prefer "Inclusion Training." Again, inclusion training acknowledges the strength diversity brings to an organization. However, it focuses on:

1. Understanding yourself, not others.

2. Finding the common between you and others; excluding outer-appearances.

We firmly believe that businesses, institutions, and organizations can attract, recruit and retain a broader mix of diverse high-talent individuals by creating a culture of inclusion versus a culture of tolerance.

Chapter 7: Education

In my early days as a manager in corporate America, I developed a very large unconscious bias towards people holding a Master's in Business Administration (MBA) degree. My bias stemmed from my belief that MBAs thought they were entitled to significantly larger starting salaries and expected an accelerated promotion through the Organization. As an aside, it is sort of funny that I hear similar comments from older managers about Millennials today!

As I look back to consciously think through my bias towards MBAs, I realize some key things about them:
- they worked very hard to achieve that degree
- the curriculum was designed to prepare them to lead in a quicker timeframe
- the financial cost they incurred to obtain it, in many cases, was substantial

- by their achievement, these were bright, self-motivated achievers

Unfortunately, the awareness of my implicit bias didn't occur until a few years into my managerial roles. I often wonder how many high-talent individuals I discarded that could have taken the company to new and higher levels. Again, as an aside, I hope if you are in a Leadership position currently, you realize your implicit biases earlier than I did!

You may want to assess your initial thoughts as they relate to others' gender, age, education, culture, ethnicity and other things that may differ from you. If any of those thoughts appear biased (negatively or positively), you may want to put some conscious thought into why you hold those beliefs.

- **Are those beliefs based on fact or fiction?**
- **Are they based on truth or opinion?**

- Are they learned beliefs or self-developed beliefs?
- Are they general stereotypes or based on the individual?

All are valid questions for any Leader to ask themselves. These are questions that I had to train myself to go through mentally as a standard practice when I interact with others; react to events; or respond to situations.

In a recent workshop, we had a young man that grew up participating in a family business. His education after high school was 100% vocational training. His view (filter), regarding college and university graduates, was that they were not that smart. To paraphrase what he shared with us, "They might know a lot about what they read in books, but they sure don't know how to make things work in the real world." His belief about academic education created an unconscious bias towards people who chose academia over vocational training. His behavior was to devalue their worth and their ability to significantly contribute.

It was interesting to watch him work through his thought process of why he felt academics were less valuable. As he kept processing this, he realized that he really didn't value the opinions or input from someone who only went through the higher education process; without ever having a "real" job. After participating in several workshop group discussions, he realized that some of those "college people" in the room had value. In addition, he found other things they had in common outside of educational backgrounds.

Today, a majority of the college and university students are women. In Chapter 6: History, we talked about the major change that occurred in opening opportunities for woman in the workforce. Those opportunities were a result of the manpower shortage created during World War II.

Many of those women chose to remain in the workforce after the war. This created the first domestic wave of females entering jobs previously "reserved" for men.

If the war created a movement of woman into the workforce, what do you think the higher ratio of females to males attending our higher learning institutions predicts for the future? Many women that previously chose family over career are now deciding they don't need to choose between the two; they can have both or either. They are entering fields such as engineering, architecture, political science, medical, etc.

As they enter their post-graduate roles as entrepreneurs, co-workers, managers, executives, etc., they will encounter the unconscious bias, of both men and other women, that they are less capable than a man with the same educational credentials. People that still hold beliefs that the best person for the job is a man.

People with these beliefs will exhibit unfavorable behavior towards these females. That behavior could show itself through a span of practices from insubordination to attempting to have the person removed from their position. This sounds a little harsh; however, women with higher education degrees should be ready for those who applaud their accomplishment, and those that believe they shouldn't be there.

- *The National Center for Education Statistics estimated that females were 57% of the 2016 U.S. college and university enrollment population.*

Chapter 8: Spiritual

Perhaps spiritual environments may be one of the strongest influencers on our implicit biases. Just by the very nature of believing, or not believing, in a higher being produces very strong views people have of each other. The belief of higher beings with different names; different origins; and different teachings also creates both explicit and implicit biases.

I grew up in the Pentecostal faith; specifically, Apostolic. The church I attended in my youth held the belief that it was the only way to heaven. Other "religions" or other spiritual beliefs could not provide you with a means of getting to Heaven; even if those beliefs were based on "Christianity." Christianity consists of many different religious groups such as the Latin Church, Catholicism, Eastern

Orthodox, Anglican Communion, Protestant, Lutheran, etc.

So, in a religion that didn't acknowledge other Christian-based beliefs, what do you think the thoughts were regarding beliefs that were not based on Christianity? Beliefs such as Baha'i, Buddhist, Confucians, Hindu, Islam, Judaism, etc. Worse yet, how about Agnostics or Atheist.

As I look back on the early religious teaching I received, I was conflicted in my beliefs. On one hand, I was told to "love thy neighbor"; on the other hand I was told if they weren't a believer of my faith "They are going to hell." This did create an early belief in me that my religion was the right one, and the only one to enter Heaven. As I began traveling domestically, and internationally, I realized there were people that felt as strongly about their religious beliefs.

As far as unconscious biases go this is probably one of the toughest categories to overcome those biases. That is because our belief, or non-belief, in a higher being strikes at the core of who we are.

I have a 15-year-old son. Right now, he is really searching for his own spiritual place. He is torn between Christianity and some of the other beliefs, such as Buddhism. He is conflicted because as he reads more about history, he realizes that many wars were fought for the sake of "Christianity." For him, there is no reconciling the two, Christianity and war. I realize that right now this has created an unconscious belief for him that Christians are warmongers, and use Christ as an excuse to leverage things for themselves. This is the filter he currently sees Christians through. While I hope and pray that he finds his path to Christianity someday, I believe my role is to help educate him on those wars; create an open and safe environment for discussions regarding his beliefs; and show him my beliefs through my actions, not through my words or directives.

The reason I shared this with you, is that is the same approach we take in our workshops. We want to create an open and safe environment to discuss religion and its role in our beliefs and the biases about others, and the effect it might have on our responses to situations and our reactions to events.

This is an area of our workshop that we really focus on respect for other's beliefs and filters (their view of others, situations, and events). We believe that if we are truly working with our clients on creating an inclusive and welcoming environment spirituality needs to be one of the workshop's group discussions.

Chapter 9: Social Exposure

Social exposure happens in many different environments. It occurs where we work, live and play. It also occurs in the clubs, associations, committees and other activities that we choose to participate.

Most people will tend to gravitate to social experiences that are more comfortable; meet an interest, or meet a requirement for them.

We often ask the participants in our workshops to think about their social interactions in terms of three concentric circles:

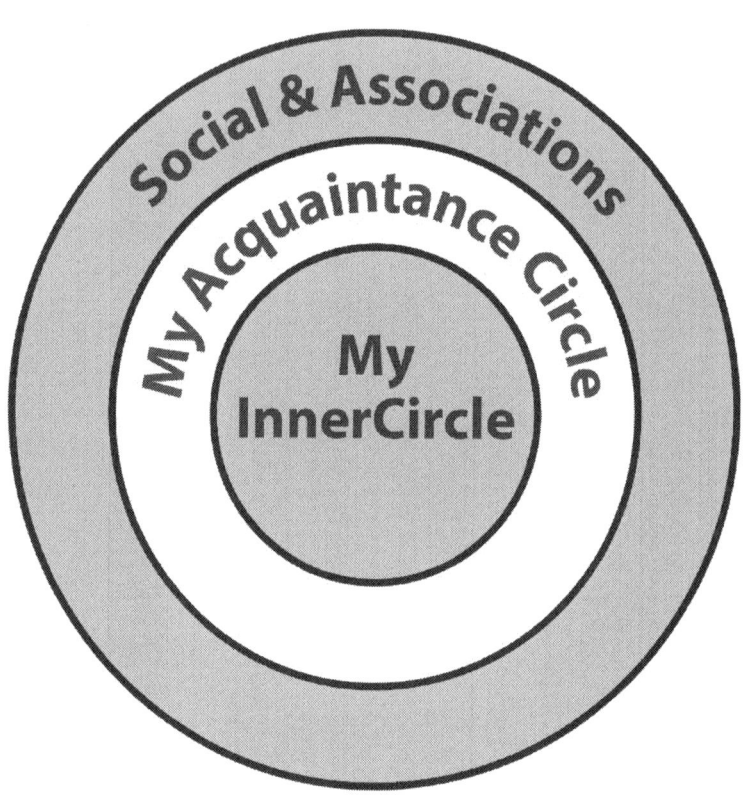

The Inner Circle – This includes those you are closest to. Family; close friends; people who are in your home on a regular basis

The Acquaintance Circle – This may include co-workers you frequently have conversations or lunch with; people you know well, but are not guests at your home; people you see and talk to often

Social and Associations – Groups or clubs you belong to; Associations you have joined

Let's start with your "Inner Circle." List the people that reside in this circle for you. What do these people look like? Race? Ethnicity? Gender?

Next, let's list the people in your "Acquaintance Circle." What do these people look like? Race? Ethnicity? Gender?

Last, let's look at your outer circle "Social & Associations." What do these groups look like? Race? Ethnicity? Gender?

The exercise you just completed is just another piece of understanding the beliefs, biases, and filters (*the way we view others, situations and events*) that each of us have. Many times, our workshop participants realize that their groups may look like them; especially their Inner Circle.

There is absolutely nothing wrong with that. This is perfectly natural for the people in our inner circle to have many things in common with us. We are just encouraging you to maybe begin including some people who don't look like you but still have many common interests with you.

When I began my corporate career, it was very easy to fill my circles with people who didn't look like me but had many common interests. The only reason this was easy for me, is because there weren't that many people of color in the industries I began my career.

This was fortunate for me because it literally forced me to include others in my circles. This is less true today because there are considerably more racially and ethnically diverse people in all industries. So, your effort to create more diversity in your circles is strictly voluntary!

Chapter 10: Media Influence

Just as the sign above suggests, there are many directions you can go to get information today! The issue is we sometimes forget the following things:

- All media outlets are trying to get high ratings to attract advertisers
- Anything written or viewed was created by someone with their own beliefs and biases

- Mass media outlets are catering to a specific audience to gain market share
- Media knows that people are attracted to excitement and conflict

When you sum all of this up, whether it's print or digital, the media's primary function is to get your attention and your repeat reading or viewing. This creates outlets with certain types of information, and with different types of cultures to attract a specific segment of the market.

It is interesting to watch two of the major network news channels, who will remain unnamed, report on the same situation or event. I compare it to two people watching the same sporting event, but the game stats and the winning team are different in each of their stories! Because the media outlets cater to specific markets, they are going to publish and report in a manner that is best liked by the individuals in that market.

A prime example would be a publication or program that is politically motivated. Politically, there is a broad spectrum of viewers and readers. As a generality, in the U.S. we have individuals who favor the far "conservative right" and individuals who favor the far "liberal left; and everyone else somewhere in between. The two unnamed news channels tend to be in opposite positions on that political spectrum. So, when you hear the same political news story, it tends to be reported very differently.

How is all of this connected to unconscious bias? Most people have one, or a few, favorite sources of information; whether those sources are internet, TV, radio, or print. If those few sources are producing biased information designed for targeting and catering to their repeat clients; then what is fact and what is entertainment. If the goal is to gain market share, attract repeat audiences and attract advertisers, then you must format your program towards your audience's beliefs.

Our point is that media outlets are designed to provide the information you want to hear, in a format you want to hear it in, and in a manner that produces the highest ratings. Always remember the people creating and delivering the information are biased also.

So, what is the solution to prevent developing my own unconscious beliefs from information that we receive from the media? My answers are a lot of research on my own; and always read, watch or listen to media sources with opposing views.

The media has a tremendous impact on the way we view the world around us <u>because they are how most of us get the information about the world around us</u>. So, if the media sources that you patronize present an inaccurate or misleading fact, that may become your belief. Even if they provide a retraction of the erroneous information, our unconscious mind has already captured the original story or report.

When these repeated stories and reports are captured in our unconscious mind, it will retrieve that information when interacting with others, or responding to an event or situation. As an example, most of us realize that <u>all</u> Muslims are not terrorists. However, I want to share a true story with you.

My Partner and I were waiting at the baggage claim carousel at Detroit's Wayne County Airport. We noticed that all the passengers from our flight were standing on the opposite side from where the luggage comes out of the conveyor belt. Usually, you would have to jockey for position to be the closest to where your luggage exits the conveyor. Anyway, we couldn't figure out why the passengers were on the other side of the carousel.

As we were standing there discussing how strange it seemed, my Partner tapped me on the shoulder and told me to look behind us. Standing directly behind us were two young Muslim women. They were in niqab and abaya apparel (*veil covering the head and face, leaving the eyes exposed; and a loose black garment covering from head to feet*). Why do you think everyone was standing on the opposite side of the luggage carousel?

I believe many of them had watched, heard or read about the several recent terror attacks, and initially, unconsciously moved to what they thought might be a safe distance from the young women.

However, for us, the two young women were typical for this location. The city of Dearborn, a Detroit suburb that is very close to the airport, may have the largest single community of Muslims in the United States.

My Partner and I cannot say for sure that these people's beliefs, biases, and behavior were affected by the media; but we did appreciate the opportunity to be closest to the luggage chute for once!

CLOSING COMMENTS

It is truly amazing how you and I have been influenced by the unique environments in which we grew up. More astonishing is how much these early environments and our individual experiences unconsciously shape our beliefs and biases as they relate to other people, situations, and events. Those unconscious, or implicit, biases play such a significant role in shaping our view of everything around us. Unfortunately, many of those biases, beliefs, and views tend to be untrue or without any real connection to facts.

Hopefully, this book is helpful in recognizing many of your own implicit biases. More importantly to help you understand the beliefs and views they may cause you to hold; especially those beliefs that are not based on fact or truth. Throughout the book, we used examples of our own implicit biases and the resulting, or possible, behaviors. Also, we shared some cases discovered by participants during our workshop training sessions. We believe these examples might provide a platform for you to think through some of your own implicit biases and help you gain a greater understanding of the possible causes.

Our Team has spent considerable time studying and understanding the impact of implicit bias as it relates to interactions between people; the reactions individuals have towards situations and events; and the possible resulting behaviors that could have tremendous effects on individual and organizational success.

Also, it is a major contributor to the organizations' ability to create a welcoming and inclusive culture. Today, a welcoming culture is crucial to being able to attract and retain the top talent from all types of backgrounds.

As one of the outputs of our research, we have developed an interactive workshop (Turning Unconscious Bias into Conscious Thought). The workshop is designed to assist individuals and organizations to think through the possibilities of their own implicit biases and the potential for undesirable and unintended consequences.

Our Team believes that implicit bias and its ramifications (positive or negative) are reflected in the success and sustainability of any company, institution or association. The key is to gain a better understanding of those biases; the causes; and determine the impact they may have on our behavior towards others and our reactions to situations and events.

With the increased acceleration in demographic changes, it is crucial to any organization's success to attract talent, build new customers and enter unfamiliar markets. Implicit biases can be an obstacle that hinders an organization from creating a welcoming culture for high-talent individuals; regardless of their differences.

The focus of our interactive workshops is to help individuals and organizations build a more welcoming culture. This process involves helping the participants develop stronger relationships with their associates, managers, clients, vendors and other key stakeholders. This is accomplished by sharing their early environments and experiences in a group setting and connecting the commonality in their stories with others in the room.

Also, there is a post-workshop activity that the participants are asked to perform that reinforces finding the common between their story and the story of others.

Thank you for allowing us to share.

About the Authors

Phil Claybrooke, President/CEO
Metrics2Results

- 25+ years of executive experience in a variety of leadership positions with IBM, Honeywell, Johnson Controls as well as employee-owned businesses.

- Leadership and facilitation roles in diversity & inclusion, cultural transition coaching and training.

M2R, Inc is extremely passionate about individuals and organizations understanding the impact that unconscious (implicit) bias can have on financial and operational success; as well as the entity's ability to attract and retain high-talent individuals.

Harvey Phelps
Executive Vice President
Metrics2Results, Inc.
Harvey has spent many years linking majority business' requirements with small businesses' services and products. He has vast experience across the spectrum of large companies; small companies; and D/V/W/MBE companies and geographic regions.

Made in the USA
Columbia, SC
29 June 2019